D1307746

MARGARITA
Rocks

MIX AND ENJOY MORE THAN **70** FABULOUS
MARGARITAS AND TEQUILA-BASED COCKTAILS

HENRY BESANT & ANDRES MASSO
PHOTOGRAPHY BY WILLIAM LINGWOOD

This book is dedicated to Mum

Margarita Rocks

First published in the United Kingdom
and Ireland in 2005 by
Duncan Baird Publishers Ltd
Sixth Floor
Castle House
75–76 Wells Street
London W1T 3QH

Conceived, created, and designed by
Duncan Baird Publishers

Copyright © Duncan Baird Publishers 2005
Text copyright © Duncan Baird Publishers 2005
Commissioned photography copyright © Duncan
Baird Publishers 2005

All rights reserved. No part of this book may be
reproduced in any form or by any electronic or
mechanical means, including information storage
and retrieval systems, without permission in writing
from the publisher, except by a reviewer who may
quote brief passages in a review.

Project Editor: Kirsten Chapman
Editorial Support: Mary Loebig Giles
Managing Designer: Dan Sturges
Commissioned Photography: William Lingwood
Prop Stylist: Helen Trent

British Library Cataloguing-in-Publication Data:
A CIP record for this book is available from the
British Library

ISBN-10: 1-84483-151-5
ISBN-13: 9-781844-831517

10 9 8 7 6 5 4 3 2 1

Typeset in Celestia Antiqua
Colour reproduction by Scanhouse, Malaysia
Printed in Singapore by Imago

Publisher's Note: The cocktails in this book
are intended for the consumption of adults,
in moderation. Neither the publishers nor
the authors can accept responsibility for any
consequences arising from the use of this book
or from the information contained therein.

CONTENTS

FOREWORD

Why has the Margarita become the most popular cocktail in the world? Part of the answer may lie in the characteristics we associate with its base spirit: tequila has a sense of fun, wildness, and edgy danger. But a more important reason has to be that the Margarita simply tastes so damn good!

Having now worked with the Margarita some 28 years, serving millions of them across six countries, we both know a fair amount about this sublime cocktail. We've learned how to mix the perfect Margarita by constantly tasting and readjusting the recipe—occasionally with such dedication that our quality-control sessions have resulted in broken tables and wrestling in the streets.

We discovered that besides using quality tequila, lime, and triple sec, all these ingredients had to be in the right proportions. When a Margarita is balanced, it refreshes from the first sip. And that's whether you're having it before food, with food, after food, or totally without food.

The Margarita has tremendous versatility, which means it suits virtually any and all occasions. But you can also play with the Margarita. You can vary the type of tequila, citrus, and sweetener used, as well as anything extra you might add, such as fruit. You have a choice of preparation methods: mixing, blending, on the rocks, straight up ... the combinations are endless.

If you're looking for a good place to learn about mixing and enjoying Margaritas, you won't find any place better than this book. The recipes are innovative and taste absolutely amazing, and they'll encourage you to go on and create your own versions of this celebrated cocktail. You'll know you've made a good Margarita when you serve it to someone, they take their first sip, and then can't resist a second or third taste before setting the glass down again. Enjoy this book, enjoy the Margaritas, enjoy tequila, and enjoy your life. To your very good health!

Julio Bermejo,
Owner, Tommy's Mexican Restaurant, San Francisco,
and Ambassador of Tequila to the US

Tomas Estes,
Owner, Café Pacifico and La Perla restaurants, worldwide,
and Ambassador of Tequila to Europe

THE STORY OF TEQUILA

The Margarita has done a lot to bring tequila in from the badlands of the drink world to a certain legitimacy. But the cocktail still draws its strength of character from tequila, a spirit that reveals the heart and soul of Mexico: raw, real life, the unexpected, and adventure.

Tequila's roots go back to pre-Columbian Mexico, to a drink made by the Aztecs and other native peoples. This drink, pulque, was produced from the juice of agave plants, which grow all over the semi-desert region. Despite their long, spiny leaves, agave are not a type of cactus, as some people believe, but a member of the lily family. Pulque was made by simply extracting the agave juice from the heart of the plant (the *piña*) and leaving it to ferment. Later, agave growers heated the juice to make a distilled drink known as mezcal—the earliest form of tequila.

Just over 200 years ago, farmers in the town of Tequila, in Jalisco state, started to refine the agave growing and distillation processes. Discovering that the blue agave (*Agave azul tequilana weber*) produced a particularly fine spirit, they began to use it as their only source of agave. At the distillery they baked the *piñas* slowly in steam ovens—rather than in underground charcoal ovens, as for mezcal. They also enhanced the quality of their drink by distilling it twice. So distinctive and delicious was the end-result that it became recognized as a spirit in itself—and so tequila was born. Tequila production methods are now strictly regulated by the Mexican government and authorized in only five Mexican states, all to ensure that the quality of tequila is preserved.

When buying tequila there are various types you can choose from:

BLANCO OR PLATA: meaning "white" and "silver," these terms refer to clear tequilas that are bottled soon after distillation.

REPOSADO: "rested" tequilas are left in oak barrels for 2 to 12 months.

AÑEJO: "aged" tequilas are allowed to mature in oak barrels for at least 12 months. Often these barrels have previously contained other spirits like bourbon or Cognac, and this adds flavor to the tequila.

Tequilas within these categories do share similar characteristics—blancos are often light, while añejos are rounded and full-bodied—but the taste of a tequila often depends more on the distillery and area in which it is produced. Tequilas from the highlands, for example, tend to have fruity notes, while lowland tequilas are generally earthy. To find a tequila you like it's best simply to try as many as you can.

100% AGAVE QUALITY

All of the tequilas mentioned above can be either "100 percent agave" or a mixto. Always check the label to see that you're buying 100 percent agave tequilas, as these are made from pure agave juice. In a mixto up to 49 percent of the alcohol may derive from other sugars. Be wary too of tequilas referred to as joven abocado; these include colorings to enhance their appearance—they're also called "gold tequila"—and tend to be mixtos.

MIXING MARGARITAS

Making Margaritas and other cocktails is like making anything else: you can throw all the ingredients together in a haphazard way, or you can assemble them with care and consideration. The method you use will be reflected in the final product. In this book all the recipes serve one, unless otherwise stated.

THE INGREDIENTS

The most important component of your Margarita is, naturally, the tequila (see previous pages). For most recipes we've suggested a type (and often a brand in brackets), which will work well with the combination of flavors. But feel free to use any tequilas you like—just make sure they're 100 percent agave (see box, page 8).

Triple sec is a clear-looking liqueur, made from the peel of sweet and bitter oranges, and it provides the sweetness in your Margarita—vary the ratio of triple sec to tequila and lime to suit your taste. Whenever possible use a good quality triple sec, with an alcohol content of 25 to 40 percent. Cointreau is a reputable brand. Grand Marnier, a Cognac-based liqueur flavored with oranges, makes a luxurious alternative.

The third major ingredient of your Margarita is the lime. Although you could use bottled juice, you can't beat the tang of freshly squeezed lime juice. Look for limes with a little give when you squeeze them—they're likely to be juicy. Dark limes tend to have a stronger flavor than lighter ones. Persian limes and Mexican limes are particularly good varieties. Avoid sour mixes; they're filled with artificial flavorings.

To your basics you can add any number of liqueurs, wines, and fruit juices as mixers, as well as herbs, spices, or edible flavorings. We've included a wide variety in our recipes, but be as creative as you like! The Flavor-mix Chart on page 116 gives further suggestions. One ingredient you should get is agave syrup. This syrup, like tequila, is made from agave juice and enhances the spirit's flavor in cocktails. Agave syrup also makes a great alternative to sugar—it's lower in carbohydrates and calories. Find agave syrup in grocery or health-food stores. (Or replace it with equal quantities of sugar syrup. For recipe, see box, page 16.)

THE TECHNIQUES

The way you mix is almost as important as what you mix. Here are a few of the basic techniques that will help you make great cocktails.

CHILLING THE GLASS: simply place the glass in a refrigerator for 15 to 20 minutes before use—or in the freezer for a frosted effect on the outside of the glass. If time is short: fill the glass with ice and cold water and leave it to stand while you mix. Don't, however, chill or frost your glass if you're salting the rim (see below), as the salt will go everywhere.

SALTING THE RIM: Margaritas are often served with a salt coating on the rim to add a further flavor profile. To do this hold the glass upside down and wipe around the rim with a wedge of lime, squeezing

THE EQUIPMENT

You don't need to go out and spend lots of cash on fancy equipment. Get these basics together and you'll be set to go:

MEASURE: also called a jigger, this is essential for following the recipes correctly when you're starting out.

SHAKER: there are two major types. The Manhattan is a three-piece shaker, made of stainless steel, which consists of a beaker, a lid with a built-in strainer, and a cap. The Boston shaker, preferred by many bartenders, comprises a glass beaker and a steel beaker—it requires a separate strainer.

STRAINERS: for our recipes we have used two types. The hawthorn strainer is a metal disk with a coil "rim;" it sits inside a cocktail shaker. The fine strainer looks like a mini seive and sits inside the glass.

MIXING GLASS: a large, sturdy glass with a lip, in which you can stir one or more servings. Or use the metal base of your cocktail shaker—many bartenders do this because metal is a good conductor of heat, so chills a drink quickly.

BAR SPOON: a small spoon with a long, twisting handle, ideal for stir-ring drinks in jugs or tall glasses. Many bar spoons have a flat disk on the other end which is perfect for muddling (see box, page 21).

SELECTION OF GLASSES: the glass most associated with cocktails is the **Martini glass** (or cocktail glass). This has a cone-shaped bowl and a long, thin stem, which allows you to hold the glass without warming your drink. The Martini glass is great for Margaritas, or you can get a dedicated **Margarita glass**. It's a similar shape to the Martini glass but more rounded, with a wider rim for salting. The **old-fashioned** is a short, straight-sided glass often used for drinks like whiskey on the rocks (it's also called a rocks glass or tumbler). For long, iced drinks invest in some **tall glasses**: the straight-sided **highball**; the taller, narrower **collins**; or the **hurricane** glass, which has a tall, rounded bowl and a short stem. Small, sturdy **shot glasses** are good for slamming or shooting tequila. For more civilized sipping select **champagne flutes**; their tall, tapering bowls help champagne keep its fizz.

the wedge slightly to get plenty of juice on the rim. Then dip the rim in a saucer of coarse-grained rock salt or kosher salt—don't use fine-grained table salt as this tastes too salty. If any salt falls into the glass, remove it with a piece of fruit or the corner of a napkin; salt should be a garnish not an ingredient. To give the drinker an option on the salt, coat only half the rim. For a sweet alternative wipe the rim with orange and dip into a saucer of sugar, shredded coconut, or cinnamon.

SHAKING: when a recipe asks you to shake, place the ingredients in your cocktail shaker, add cubed ice almost to the rim, seal, and shake vigorously. Don't be delicate, shake like you really mean it, but 10 to 20 seconds is long enough; if you shake for too long, the ice will over-dilute the cocktail. To refine your shaking style, watch a good bar-tender, perhaps even take your shaker to him or her and ask for lessons.

STIRRING AND BLENDING: stirred drinks are made in a mixing glass, in the base of the cocktail shaker, or sometimes in the glass itself,

TRICKS AND TIPS

* Keep all drinks in a cool place.
* Work on a surface that can be wiped down easily.
* Wash your equipment between each type of cocktail. And always use fresh ice so that you don't taint the flavor of the new drink.
* The more ice you use, the cooler the drink. Cubed ice is often best as it doesn't dilute the drink too much. But crushed ice is useful for cooling a drink quickly or for blending (see page 13).
* Taste the cocktail before you serve it, using a teaspoon or by dipping a straw in and covering the top of the straw with your finger to capture a drop of liquid.
* Follow the recipe at first, but don't be afraid to experiment.

as the recipe requires. Again, when stirring add plenty of ice—almost to the rim. Stir 30 or 40 times; this is enough to mix the ingredients and chill the drink, but not so long that the drink becomes watery. If you are mixing in a metal shaker, you'll know the drink is cool enough when condensation appears on the outside of the shaker. For blended drinks just whiz the ingredients together in a blender with crushed ice—not cubed, as it will ruin the motor of your blender.

STRAINING: if your cocktail consists mostly of liquid ingredients, it's usually enough to single strain it. This involves using just the built-in strainer of a three-piece cocktail shaker or a hawthorn strainer (see page 11) on top of a Boston shaker. If the drink contains solid ingredients or you've shaken it hard, it's often better to double strain to get rid of flecks of fruit, herbs, or broken ice. This means that you strain the drink through the built-in strainer or hawthorn strainer plus a fine strainer—or tea strainer—on top of the glass. If you want to serve the drink with ice, it's best to add fresh ice to the glass before you pour.

GARNISHING: a garnish not only makes the cocktail look attractive but often also adds flavor. Aside from the salt rim (see page 10), Margaritas go well with a simple citrus curl. To make this use a sharp knife to pare off a thin piece of the outer skin of an unwaxed orange (or lime or lemon), then drop it in the drink. Try not to get any of the white pith, as this has a bitter taste. For a longer, thinner twist, use a zester to remove a long, continuous strip of the skin. Berries, cherries, or fruit pieces make good garnishes for fruity drinks; while creamy drinks look delicious topped with flakes of cinnamon or chocolate.

CLASSIC &
Refined

There are many ways to make a Margarita,
and here we present our definitive mix. It's been
tried, tested, and perfected and will forever stand
the test of time. But the fun doesn't end there: for
tequila pleasure without measure, we've taken
classics, like the Mojito and the Daiquiri,
and re-mixed them Mexican style.

GLASS	1¼oz (35ml) blanco tequila (Herradura)
old-fashioned	½oz (15ml) triple sec
	½oz (15ml) fresh lime juice
GARNISH	Dash fresh lemon juice
half salt rim	1 teaspoon sugar syrup
and lime zest	

THE CLASSIC MARGARITA

For our definitive Margarita, we suggest a great example of 100 percent agave white tequila. Herradura is from the highlands, which gives the base spirit a robust and almost fruity flavor. And to show off these characteristics in the best possible way, we've combined it with ingredients that achieve a zesty, clean, and well-balanced Margarita. We've also added a dash of fresh lemon juice to bring out the citrus notes.

Pour all the ingredients into a cocktail shaker in the order listed above. Fill with cubed ice and shake well. To salt the rim of the glass, wipe a lime wedge around half the rim and the outside of the glass just below this. Dip the glass into a saucer of rock salt at an angle so that the salt coats the side of the glass as well as the rim. Fill the glass with fresh cubed ice and double strain the drink over the ice. Float a few small strips of lime zest on the top and serve.

TRICKS AND TIPS

You can buy sugar syrup or make your own. Mix 2 cups (400g) superfine (caster) sugar and 1 cup (225ml) water in a pan. Stir over a medium heat until the sugar has dissolved. Allow to cool, then transfer to a bottle or jug. You can use the mix immediately, or it will keep for weeks if sealed.

GLASS	1½oz (45ml) blanco tequila (Tapatío)
Martini	½oz (15ml) Cointreau
	2 lime wedges
GARNISH	¾oz (25ml) red cranberry juice (or white)
orange curl	

Rude Cosmopolitan

In recent years the "Cosmo" has become one of the world's most recognizable cocktails. Substituting the usual vodka base for tequila gives it greater complexity and depth. You could use white cranberry juice in place of red: it not only gives the drink a completely different appearance, but also softens the overall flavor, making it more rounded.

Chill a Martini glass. Place all the ingredients in a cocktail shaker in the order listed above—give the lime wedges a good squeeze over the shaker before you drop them in. Fill with cubed ice and shake well. Double strain into the Martini glass. Float a curl of orange zest in the top and serve.

12 fresh mint leaves	**GLASS**
1¾oz (50ml) any tequila	**tall**
¾oz (25ml) fresh lime juice	
½oz (15ml) sugar syrup	**GARNISH**
	mint sprig

Menta

Even while you're mixing this, the smell of the mint will blow you away. The Menta is a variation of Cuba's most famous cocktail and one of Ernest Hemingway's favorite tipples: the Mojito. This drink works amazingly well with any style of tequila, so we've left it up to you to decide. Whatever you choose the result will be incredibly refreshing—great for cooling down after an energetic salsa!

Gather the mint in your hand and hold it tight between your fingers and thumb. Rub the herb around the inside edge of a tall glass to release the mint aroma. Give the leaves a single tear and drop them into the glass. Cover with a bed of crushed ice (about half the glass). Add the remaining ingredients and muddle together (see below) with a muddler or the flat end of a bar spoon. Fill the glass with more crushed ice to the rim. Top with a luscious mint sprig and serve.

TRICKS AND TIPS

Muddling is a vital cocktail-making skill. It involves grinding fruits, herbs, spices, etc. to release their natural flavors into your mix. You can muddle the ingredients in the bottom of your glass, a mixing glass, or in the base of a cocktail shaker. Use the flat end of a bar spoon, a muddler (a cocktail tool that looks like a thin pestle), or the end of a small rolling pin.

GLASS Martini or old-fashioned
GARNISH none

1 teaspoon agave syrup
1 teaspoon sugar syrup
1 teaspoon still mineral water
1³/₄oz (50ml) any tequila
³/₄oz (25ml) fresh lime juice

TOMMY'S MARGARITA

This mix is inspired by the legendary Tommy's Restaurant in San Francisco. Tommy's lays claim to one of the largest selections of tequila outside Mexico; here you can sample over 200 different 100 percent agave tequilas. This recipe is based on the classic Margarita, but we've dropped the orange liqueur in favor of an agave syrup mix to accentuate the flavor of the base spirit. Experiment with different tequilas and take time over the results. This is the ultimate Margarita for tequila lovers.

Chill a Martini or old-fashioned glass. Pour the agave syrup, sugar syrup, and mineral water into a cocktail shaker. Stir well, until thoroughly combined. Add the remaining ingredients. Fill with cubed ice and shake well. Double strain into the glass and serve.

GLASS Martini
GARNISH maraschino cherry

1³/₄oz (50ml) añejo tequila (Chinaco)
¹/₂oz (15ml) sweet vermouth
Dash maraschino syrup (or the juice
    that comes with your cherries)
4 drops Angostura bitters
Piece of orange zest

SWEET MEXICAN MANHATTAN

The classic Manhattan—consisting of whiskey, vermouth, and bitters—is over 120 years old and was said to have originated at the Manhattan Club in New York. Manhattan drinkers today often tailor the recipe to suit their taste, drinking it sweet, medium, or dry. For our tequila-based version, we've chosen to use sweet vermouth because it really complements the flavors of a good, aged tequila.

Chill a Martini glass. Fill a mixing glass with cubed ice. Pour all the ingredients except the orange zest over the ice. Stir well for about 30 seconds, allowing the ice to dilute the mixture slightly. Single strain into the Martini glass. Squeeze the orange zest over the glass to release the oils into the drink, then discard the zest. Drop a cherry in the drink and serve.

GLASS old-fashioned or champagne flute
GARNISH lemon twist and a cherry
1³⁄₄oz (50ml) plata tequila (Gran Centenario)
³⁄₄oz (25ml) fresh lemon juice
¹⁄₂oz (15ml) sugar syrup
4 drops Angostura bitters
1 teaspoon egg white (optional)

BLANCA

This recipe is based on the "Sour" mix, which works well with most spirits— and even liqueurs—but is perhaps most commonly found in conjunction with whiskey. Combined with tequila it produces a heady libation in which the sour elements mingle with the floral and spicy notes of the base spirit. If you include an egg white, your drink will have a smoother consistency and a foamy head.

Pour all the ingredients into a cocktail shaker. Fill with cubed ice and shake well. Fill an old-fashioned glass with fresh cubed ice and double strain the mix over the ice. Drop a lemon twist and a cherry in the top and serve. Alternatively, serve without ice in a chilled champagne flute.

1³/₄oz (50ml) reposado tequila (Porfidio)
4 to 6 drops Tabasco sauce
8 drops Worcestershire sauce
Pinch of celery salt
Pinch of ground black pepper
¹/₂ teaspoon ground horseradish
2 teaspoons fresh lemon juice
1 cup (225ml) tomato juice

GLASS
large old-fashioned
or tall

GARNISH
black pepper rim
and thin celery strips

Bloody Maria

Another variation on a classic—this time the Bloody Mary. But unlike the vodka version, you'll get a sense of the **tequila's full character** among the other ingredients. The **spice** mix that we've suggested will give good **intensity** and **heat**. But if you prefer **something a bit stronger**, feel free to experiment. Adding another flavor such as garlic, cumin, or cilantro (coriander) creates an **interesting complexity**.

Wipe the rim of an old-fashioned glass with a lemon wedge and dip into a dish of freshly ground black pepper. Fill the glass with cubed ice. Build the ingredients over the ice in the order listed above. Stir well with a bar spoon. Top up with cubed ice if necessary. Garnish with thin strips of celery and serve.

TRICKS AND TIPS

Adding a crown of dry sherry or red wine can turn this into a real winter warmer. Mix the drink as above, but leave a little space at the top. Gently pour the sherry or wine over the flat end of a bar spoon to create a rich crown floating on the drink.

GLASS	1 white sugar cube
champagne flute	4 to 5 drops Angostura bitters
	$^{3}/_{4}$oz (25ml) añejo tequila (1800)
GARNISH	$^{1}/_{2}$ cup (100ml) champagne
long orange curl	

THE ROYAL

This mix is based on the Classic Champagne Cocktail, but we've substituted the Cognac for tequila to produce a queen among Margaritas. It's a fabulous mix of dry champagne, earthy tequila, the tang of orange, and a hint of bitters, which gets sweeter as you get closer to the sugar cube at the bottom— the simple way to bring a touch of class to any party!

Pre-chill a champagne flute. Place a sugar cube on a disposable napkin and douse with several drops of Angostura bitters. Transfer the cube into the flute. Add the tequila and fill to the top with champagne. Pare off a long, thick curl of orange zest. Wipe around the rim of the glass and squeeze over the top of the drink to release the oils, then drop it in, and serve.

100% FACT

There are many stories about where the Margarita originated. One of the earliest claims that in 1938 a showgirl called Marjorie King—who was allergic to all alcohol except tequila—asked for a cocktail at the Rancho del Gloria Bar in Rosarita Beach, Mexico. The bartender translated Marjorie's name into Spanish and named the mix in her honor.

GLASSES shots
GARNISH none
3³/₄ cups (850ml) tomato juice
³/₄oz (25ml) Tabasco sauce
¹/₂ cup (100ml) fresh lime juice
2 teaspoons rock salt

SANGRITA PITCHER

If you ask for a shot of tequila in Mexico, you may also get a shot of Sangrita. We encourage people to have this non-alcoholic chaser rather than the more usual lime and salt, as the sangrita cools you with fruit juice after the burn of the alcohol, aiding digestion and preventing you from getting too drunk! There are various Sangrita recipes, but this one, given to us by a Mexican artist called Miguel, is our favorite. To spice it up add a little Worcestershire sauce or, for something fruitier, replace some of the tomato juice with orange and pomegranate juice. This recipe makes 16 to 22 shots.

Place all the ingredients in a large jug. Stir well. Cover and refrigerate for at least one hour, but preferably overnight. Serve in shot glasses—one shot of Sangrita for each shot of tequila.

GLASS Martini
GARNISH raspberry
1¹/₂oz (40ml) reposado tequila (El Tesoro)
³/₄oz (25ml) dark crème de cacao
¹/₂oz (15ml) crème de framboise
2 teaspoons heavy (double) cream

SILK STOCKINGS

A classic cocktail from the roaring '20s, this is one of the few tequila recipes that has stood the test of time. The mix of crème de cacao and cream brings the chocolate notes of the tequila to the fore where they marry beautifully with the fruit liqueur. The cocktail was created in honor of the ladies of the time whose hemlines were rising, allowing a sexy glimpse of silk stockings. Smooth, rich, and creamy, it's a deliciously naughty drink that slides down smoothly with a bit of after-dinner jazz.

Chill a Martini glass. Pour all the ingredients into a cocktail shaker. Fill with cubed ice and shake well. Double strain the mix into the Martini glass. Place a raspberry on the rim and serve.

GLASS collins or highball
GARNISH lemon slice
1³/₄oz (50ml) reposado tequila
   (Jose Cuervo Tradicional)
³/₄oz (25ml) fresh lemon juice
¹/₂oz (15ml) sugar syrup
²/₃ cup (150ml) soda water

JOSÉ COLLINS

The Collins is one of the first cocktails
you should try to make, as a well-made
one perfectly demonstrates balance. It
is also a drink that's soured, sweetened,
strengthened, and lengthened, so giving
you an insight into various arts of the
bartender. The base spirit of a Collins
cocktail determines its first name: a
Tom Collins is gin based, a Mick Collins
contains Irish whiskey, a Jo Collins is
vodka based, while a Pedro Collins
contains white rum. Some people call a
tequila-based Collins a Pepito, but we
thought that José might be more
appropriate, particularly if you use the
nicely balanced Jose Cuervo Tradicional.

Fill a highball or collins glass with ice.
Build the ingredients over the ice in the
order listed above. Stir gently, so you don't
lose the fizz from the soda water. Drop a
slice of lemon in the drink and serve.

1 teaspoon sugar syrup
6 drops Angostura bitters
1³/₄oz (50ml) añejo tequila
(Jose Cuervo Reserva de la Familia)

GLASS
old-fashioned

GARNISH
orange curl

Estilo Viejo

The classic Old-Fashioned—which shares its name with the glass in which it's served—is a whiskey cocktail first created in the early 20th century by a Bourbon whiskey distiller and a bartender from Louisville, Kentucky. The Old-Fashioned is a favorite with bartenders all over the world, as it takes time, effort, and love to make, and really shows off your skills. For our version we recommend that you use a good quality aged tequila: Jose Cuervo Reserva de la Familia, taken from the family's private reserve, is one of the best around. Whatever you do don't rush this cocktail—when mixing or drinking it!

Pour the sugar syrup and bitters into the base of an old-fashioned glass. Add one ice cube and stir until you have a smooth paste. Add half the tequila and two more ice cubes. Stir for about 30 seconds. Add the rest of the tequila and two more ice cubes and stir well for another 30 seconds. Add more ice to fill to the rim if required. Cut a large curl of orange zest. Wipe the zest around the rim of the glass, squeeze it over the top of the drink to release the oils, then drop it in. Serve.

GLASS	1³⁄₄oz (50ml) reposado tequila (Jose Cuervo Tradicional)
tall	³⁄₄oz (25ml) fresh lime juice
	2 drops Angostura bitters (optional)
GARNISH	¹⁄₂oz (15ml) sugar syrup
3 to 4 thin	¹⁄₂ cup (100ml) ginger beer
lime wheels	

EL BURRO

This is a **Moscow Mule Mexican-style**. We've suggested that you use Jose Cuervo Tradicional as it has a **fiery** undertone that blends **perfectly** with the **tart lime** and **zesty ginger**. It's a **drink with a kick** that will carry anyone through a **blazing hot day.**

Fill a tall glass with cubed ice. Build the ingredients over the ice in the order listed above. Stir well with a bar spoon. For the garnish cut a few slices from a whole lime. Slide the slices down the inside of the glass. Top up with cubed ice if necessary and serve.

100% FACT

In Tommy's Restaurant, San Francisco, they use a staggering 4,500 pounds (2 tons) of Persian limes every month, all for Margaritas. That's the weight of a four-wheel-drive SUV. Tommy's uses around 234,000 limes a year for your favorite drink—all freshly squeezed by hand every day.

GLASS tall
GARNISH lime wedge
1³⁄₄oz (50ml) plata tequila (El Charro Silver)
³⁄₄oz (25ml) fresh lime juice
2 teaspoons sugar syrup
²⁄₃ cup (150ml) ginger ale
2 teaspoons crème de cassis

EL DIABLO

One of the earliest-listed tequila
cocktails, the Diablo was thought to
have originated in California in the
early '40s. It's quick and easy to
make as well as being wonderfully
palatable, so is the ideal party drink.
The black currant flavor of crème
de cassis can sometimes be very
powerful, so it's good to balance it
with a strong-charactered tequila
such as El Charro Silver.

Fill a tall glass with ice. Build all the ingredients except the crème de cassis over the
ice in the order listed above. Add more ice
if necessary. Pour the crème de cassis slowly in the top, to create a purple bleeding
effect through the drink. Don't stir.
Squeeze a lime wedge over the top, drop it
in, and serve.

GLASS Martini
GARNISH cherry
1³⁄₄oz (50ml) plata tequila
  (Gran Centenario)
³⁄₄oz (25ml) pink grapefruit juice
Dash fresh lime juice
2 teaspoons sugar syrup
Dash maraschino liqueur

MARGARITA HEMINGWAY

The Hemingway Daiquiri was created
for Ernest Hemingway at La Floridita
bar in Havana, Cuba. The novelist and
legendary drinker, who was in the
area writing and game fishing, had
concluded that La Floridita's Daiquiris
were good but not quite strong enough.
The owner, Constante Ribalaigua,
mixed a special strong Daiquiri which
he nicknamed the Papa Doble in honor
of Hemingway's fondness for doubles.
For our version we've substituted the
rum for a rich and elegant tequila.

Chill a Martini glass. Place all the ingredients in a blender with a cup of crushed ice.
Blend for about 30 seconds, until the drink
has a sorbet-like consistency. Pour into the
glass (no need to strain). Place a cherry on
top and serve.

GLASS tall or sling
GARNISH lime wedge and a cherry
$1^{3}/_{4}$oz (50ml) blanco tequila (Tapatío)
2 teaspoons Cherry Heering
   (or any cherry liqueur)
2 teaspoons Bénédictine
$^{1}/_{2}$oz (15ml) fresh lime juice
Dash sugar syrup
3oz (90ml) soda water

JALISCO SLING

The Singapore Sling, made with gin as a base, has been a classic cocktail since its invention at the Long Bar of the Raffles Hotel, Singapore, in around 1915. It works just as well, if not better, with tequila. We recommend Tapatío Blanco which has cinnamon notes that give the drink a light, fresh zing. If you have one, serve this in a dedicated sling glass.

Fill a tall or sling glass with cubed ice. Build all the ingredients except the soda water over the ice. Stir. Top up with soda water and more ice if necessary. Drop a lime wedge and a fresh cherry in the drink, and serve.

GLASS
old-fashioned

1³/₄oz (50ml) plata tequila (Patrón Silver)

1oz (30ml) fresh lemon juice

¹/₂oz (15ml) sugar syrup

GARNISH
lemon slice and a
blackberry

Dash crème de mûre

Scramble

This Margarita is based on The Bramble—a gin-based cocktail created by one of today's best bartenders, the London legend Dick Bradsell. Although it tastes very different from the original, this variation works beautifully. Don't stir it too much and you'll notice how each sip is unique, as the tequila, citrus, and berry flavors tumble around your mouth.

Half fill an old-fashioned glass with crushed ice and pour the tequila, lemon, and sugar syrup over the ice. Stir briefly, then fill with more crushed ice to the rim. Gently crown the cocktail (see page 25) with the crème de mûre, creating a bleeding effect through the drink. Garnish with a blackberry and a slice of lemon on the rim, and serve.

SPICY &
Aromatic

A selection of sensational spice fusions to
make the taste buds tingle. Sprinkled, dusted,
or crushed, hints of chili pepper, ginger root,
basil, or vanilla will make your Margaritas taste
divine. Some mixes are fiery, some smooth,
some a pure drop of tropical paradise, but
all will leave you wanting more ...

1in (2cm) red chili pepper, chopped

1 teaspoon sugar syrup

1³/₄oz (50ml) añejo tequila (Herradura)

³/₄oz (25ml) cloudy apple juice

³/₄oz (25ml) fresh lime juice

¹/₂oz (15ml) pomme vert (apple liqueur)

GLASS
Martini

GARNISH
slice of chili pepper
with stalk attached

Fuego Manzana

This is an appealing combination of fruit and spice that will delight to the very last drop. We have chosen Herradura Añejo due to its full-bodied oakiness, which more than holds its own against the spiciness of the chili pepper. The addition of apple provides a complex freshness and extra fruitiness to the finished cocktail. It's an award-winning drink that was created by mad-cap genius Danny Smith, one of London's top bartenders and a man who practically grew up on tequila and Margaritas.

Chill a Martini glass. Place the chili pepper and sugar syrup in a cocktail shaker. Muddle with the flat end of a bar spoon or the end of a rolling pin. Add the remaining ingredients in the order listed above. Fill with cubed ice and shake well for at least 10 seconds to infuse the mix fully with the chili pepper. Add four or five fresh cubes of ice to the Martini glass and double strain the drink over the ice—make sure that no flecks of chili get into the final drink. Cut a short flap in the side of the chili pepper slice and hang on the rim of the glass. Serve.

GLASS	1¼oz (35ml) plata tequila (Patrón Silver)
Martini	1¼oz (35ml) rose petal liqueur (Lanique)
	1¼oz (35ml) lychee juice
GARNISH	3 to 4 drops Peychaud bitters
pansy head	

FLORITA

This is a wonderfully intense and exotic libation whose flavors literally dance on the palate. We recommend that you use Lanique Rose Petal Liqueur, with its crushed rose perfume and luscious syrupy consistency, but you could substitute it with any floral liqueur. Enhanced with a flower garnish, this is one of the most appealing-looking drinks around—we've used a pansy, but rose petals, orange blossoms, or violets are also edible.

Chill a Martini glass. Pour all the ingredients into a mixing glass. Fill with cubed ice. Stir well, at least 20 times to allow the drink to chill and the ice to dilute it slightly. Single strain the mix into the Martini glass. Float the flower of your choice on top and serve.

100% FACT

Antoine Peychaud, an apothecary in early 19th-century New Orleans, created his bitter mix of herbs and spices as a flavoring and health tonic. He would often mix it with brandy, and this later evolved into the Sazerac, a drink which some claim as the original cocktail.

GLASS Martini
GARNISH basil leaf
5 basil leaves
1³/₄oz (50ml) reposado tequila (El Tesoro)
¹/₂oz (15ml) sugar syrup
³/₄oz (25ml) cloudy apple juice

TOSCANO

Particular tastes can remind you of particular places, and this is a mix that transports you straight to Italy. We came up with the recipe while on vacation in a remote farmhouse on the border of Tuscany and Umbria. The inspiration and the ingredients came from the garden around us. We made our own apple juice, picked handfuls of fresh basil—the smell of which fills the air in that part of the world—and we added sugar and tequila, a bottle of which we always have handy! Serve this cocktail with a salad of vine-ripened tomatoes and buffalo mozzarella, and you'll soon be in Italy too.

Chill a Martini glass. Tear the basil leaves and drop into the base of a cocktail shaker. Add the remaining ingredients. Fill with cubed ice and shake well. Double strain into the Martini glass, garnish with a basil leaf, and serve.

GLASS Martini
GARNISH pineapple leaf
4 cardamom pods
¹/₂ thick slice fresh pineapple
Dash sugar syrup
1³/₄oz (50ml) reposado tequila (Herradura)
Dash pineapple juice

PINEAPPLE AND CARDAMOM MARGARITA

Here the delicate but piercing flavor of cardamom combines magically with the sweetness of the pineapple to create one of our favorite recipes from this collection. This exotic libation never fails to surprise even the most adventurous of cocktail drinkers, as the initial sweetness is replaced with a light floral spiciness that lingers forever.

Chill a Martini glass. Place the cardamom pods in a cocktail shaker and crush with the flat end of a bar spoon. Chop the pineapple into chunks and add to the shaker with the syrup. Muddle well. Add the remaining ingredients. Fill with cubed ice and shake well. Double strain into the Martini glass. Cut a slit in the pineapple leaf and place on the rim of the glass. Serve.

GLASS Martini
GARNISH none
1¼oz (35ml) vanilla-infused tequila
  (see below)
½oz (15ml) triple sec
½oz (15ml) fresh lime juice
1 teaspoon sugar syrup

VANILLARITA

A deliciously fragrant alternative to the classic Margarita. Fresh vanilla accentuates the naturally sweet notes of tequila to give you a particularly palatable cocktail, which will impress even the most ardent member of the anti-tequila brigade.

Chill a Martini glass. Pour all the ingredients into a cocktail shaker. Fill with cubed ice and shake well. Double strain into the Martini glass and serve.

TRICKS AND TIPS

For vanilla-infused tequila, slice two vanilla beans lengthwise and place in a bottle of tequila. Seal and leave to stand in a warm place for 7 to 10 days. Then remove the vanilla beans to prevent their tannins from turning the tequila bitter. To accelerate the process, seal the cap of the bottle with waterproof tape, place it in your dishwasher, and run a cycle or two. The tequila will be ready in around a day.

¹/₂ thick slice pineapple
1 teaspoon agave syrup (or sugar syrup)
1³/₄oz (50ml) reposado tequila (Herradura)
³/₄oz (25ml) sage liqueur (see below)
¹/₂oz (15ml) fresh lime juice

GLASS
Martini

GARNISH
sage leaf

Sweet Sage and Pine

Sage and pineapple is an unusual combination but it's a flavor-match made in heaven. The agave syrup adds to the rich sweetness of this Margarita and binds all the ingredients. The lime juice gives the whole drink a big lift. If you can't find sage liqueur and don't have time to prepare it in advance—at least eight days before—simply muddle six fresh sage leaves with 1oz (30ml) triple sec and 1 teaspoon sugar syrup.

Chill a Martini glass. Chop the slice of pineapple into small chunks and transfer to a cocktail shaker. Add the agave syrup and muddle well. Add the remaining ingredients. Fill with cubed ice and shake well. Double strain into the Martini glass. Garnish with the sage leaf and serve.

TRICKS AND TIPS

To make your own sage liqueur—a delicious Mediterranean-style aperitif—you need: 1 bunch fresh sage, 3 cups (750ml) eau-de-vie or 100-proof vodka, and 1 cup (250ml) sugar syrup. Place the leaves in a large jug or bottle and add the alcohol. Cover and leave in a warm place for eight days. Strain into a clean bottle. Add the sugar syrup, seal, and gently shake.

GLASS **Martini or teacup**	1¼oz (35ml) reposado tequila (Espolon) ¾oz (25ml) rosehip and hibiscus tea (see below) ½oz (15ml) triple sec
GARNISH **pansy head**	½oz (15ml) fresh lime juice

ROSEHIP AND HIBISCUS MARGARITA

A delicate but exceptionally delicious Margarita—a perfect party drink with bags of sex appeal. Here we have used Espolon Reposado because of its smoothness and rounded character, which support the delicate flower flavors. And if you want to present your guests with something slightly unusual, why not serve this in bone-china teacups?

Chill a Martini glass or teacup. Pour all the ingredients into a mixing glass. Fill with cubed ice and stir gently for about 15 seconds. Single strain into the Martini glass or teacup. Float a pansy head on the top and serve. Alternatively, use any edible flower, such as rose petals, poppies, or daisies.

TRICKS AND TIPS

To make rosehip and hibiscus tea, add 6 rosehip and hibiscus teabags to 1 pint (500ml) of boiling water and steep for 6 to 8 minutes. Remove bags and stir with 1oz (30ml) honey. Allow to cool. Sealed and refrigerated, this keeps for up to one week.

GLASS sling or tall
GARNISH lime wedge and lemongrass
2in (5cm) piece lemongrass, chopped
1³/₄oz (50ml) reposado tequila (Herradura)
³/₄oz (25ml) fresh lime juice
¹/₂oz (15ml) coconut syrup
³/₄oz (25ml) apple juice
³/₄oz (25ml) pineapple juice
¹/₂ cup (100ml) ginger ale

CANCUN COOLER

Cancun's ancient Mayan ruins and white-sand beaches leading into the Caribbean Sea have attracted travelers from all over the world. We wanted to create a drink that reflected the area's vacation atmosphere and used its indigenous spirit—tequila. Use Herradura Reposado if you can for its unique freshness and hints of exotic spices and caramel.

Place the lemongrass in a cocktail shaker and smash with the flat end of a bar spoon. Add the remaining ingredients except the ginger ale. Fill with cubed ice and shake well. Half fill a tall glass with fresh cubed ice and double strain the drink over the ice. Top up with ginger ale. Squeeze the lime wedge over the drink and drop in. Float strings of lemongrass on top and serve.

GLASS champagne flute
GARNISH none
1³/₄oz (50ml) blanco tequila (Tapatío)
1oz (30ml) peppered honey and peach syrup (see below)
¹/₂ cup (100ml) champagne

HONEY AND PEACH FIZZ

When you pick up a peach, you may not naturally reach for the black pepper, but they make a surprisingly good combination. Be prepared for the syrup and champagne to react in a foamy explosion!

Pre-chill a champagne flute. Pour the tequila and the honey and peach mix into the flute (no need to strain). Add the champagne a little at a time, waiting for the bubbles to settle between each pour. Serve.

TRICKS AND TIPS

For the honey and peach syrup, you need: ¹/₂ cup (100ml) of honey; ¹/₂ cup (100ml) of hot, but not boiling, water; two peaches, peeled and chopped; and a tablespoon of black peppercorns. Blend carefully, holding the lid with a cloth. Strain the mix through a fine sieve. Bottle and refrigerate. This will keep for one week.

GLASS Martini
GARNISH strips of red bell pepper
1^3/$_4$oz (50ml) reposado tequila
   (Jose Cuervo Tradicional)
^{1}/$_2$oz (15ml) Cointreau
^{3}/$_4$oz (25ml) fresh lime juice
^{3}/$_4$oz (25ml) roasted pepper syrup (see below)

BELL PEPPER MARGARITA

There's a bar in Manchester, UK, called Socio Rehab which is an Aladdin's cave of alcoholic beverages. One of the skillful bartenders there, David Hobbs, created this spicy mix for us—we drank four each when we visited.

Chill a Martini glass. Pour all the ingredients into a cocktail shaker. Fill with cubed ice and shake well. Double strain into the glass. Top with bell pepper strips and serve.

TRICKS AND TIPS

For the bell pepper syrup, remove the heads of two red bell peppers. Sprinkle a pinch of black pepper and a little olive oil inside, and roast for 30 to 40 minutes. Mix 1 cup (200g) granulated sugar with ^{2}/$_3$ cup (150ml) tequila in a pan over medium heat. Once the sugar has dissolved, chop the bell peppers and add to the pan. Cook in a pan over low heat for 1 hour. Leave to cool, then pass through a fine sieve.

1 baby beet (beetroot), cooked and diced
2 teaspoons sugar syrup
Pinch of sea salt
1³/₄oz (50ml) blanco tequila (Arette)
2 teaspoons fresh thyme leaves

GLASS
Martini

GARNISH
salt rim and
thyme sprig

BEET AND THYME MARGARITA

Beet is a tricky ingredient to work with, but well worth the effort as this drink is spectacular if made correctly and with the right beet—small, sweet ones are best. If you are using the canned variety, be sure to wash the vegetable well to remove any brine used for pickling. Try Arette Blanco with this mix; its floral notes blend beautifully with the thyme. The whole combination works well with meat dishes, particularly lamb. A big thank you goes to Pier Paulo Dante from the London Academy of Bartending for inspiring this mix and for giving us plenty of laughs on a particular journey we shared ...

Place the beet, sugar syrup, and salt in a cocktail shaker. Muddle well, until they form a pulp. Add the tequila and thyme leaves. Fill with cubed ice and shake well. Coat the rim of a Martini glass with salt. Double strain the mix into the glass. Rest the thyme sprig on the top and serve.

GLASS	1 fresh lavender bud (not too dry)
Martini	1¼oz (35ml) blanco tequila (Tapatío)
	½oz (15ml) parfait amour
GARNISH	1 teaspoon crème de pêche
lavender sprig	2 teaspoons sugar syrup

Lavenderita

Parfait amour is a purple-colored perfumed liqueur made from and tasting of Spanish oranges, roses, and violets. Combined with the floral notes of the lavender, it has a magical effect on the tequila, naturally enhancing its herbaceous spirit. Sit back as you sip and imagine the heady scent of flowers wafting on a summer's breeze ...

Chill a Martini glass. Place the lavender bud in the base of a cocktail shaker and smash with the flat end of a bar spoon. Add the remaining ingredients. Fill with cubed ice and shake well. Double strain into the Martini glass. Float a sprig of lavender on top and serve.

100% FACT

Bottles of tequila never contain a "worm." Some bottles of mezcal—a Mexican cousin of tequila—do contain a *gusano*, which means "worm," but this is, in fact, a moth larva. These creatures have been eaten as a local delicacy for centuries.

¹/₂ small green chili pepper
8 fresh cilantro (coriander) leaves
1in (2cm) lemongrass
¹/₂in (1cm) ginger root or galangal
2 teaspoons coconut cream
2 lime wedges
1³/₄oz (50ml) reposado tequila (Don Julio)

GLASS
champagne saucer

GARNISH
lemongrass and
chili pepper knot

Phi Phi Delight

The ingredients of this Margarita—with the exception of the tequila—are present in a large number of **South-East Asian dishes**. Enjoy this with sweet or spicy Oriental food for a **taste of tropical paradise**. When making large quantities, you'll have a lot of chopping to do, so be sure to **prepare** the ingredients **in advance**.

Chill the champagne saucer. Finely chop the chili pepper, cilantro, lemongrass, and ginger root. Place in a cocktail shaker with the coconut cream. Give the lime wedges a good squeeze over the shaker and drop them in. Crush together with the flat end of a bar spoon or the end of a rolling pin. Add the tequila. Fill with cubed ice and shake well. Double strain into the champagne saucer. To garnish peel a strip of lemongrass and tie in a loose knot, then insert fine strips of chili pepper into the knot. Serve.

100% FACT

The broad, shallow champagne saucer—also called a coupe—is sometimes known as a Marie Antoinette glass. Legend has it that she had the glasses fashioned from casts of her breasts.

GLASS Martini
GARNISH dusting of smoked paprika
1in piece chili pepper, chopped
1¹/₄oz (35ml) reposado tequila
  (Gran Centenario)
¹/₂oz (15ml) Agavero (tequila liqueur)
2 teaspoons fresh lemon juice
2 teaspoons fresh lime juice
¹/₂oz (15ml) coconut cream
³/₄oz (25ml) mango purée (see page 69)

EL MARIACHI

Throughout Mexico life is accompanied
by the music of *mariachi*. These
groups combine violins, trumpets, gui-
tars, and a round-backed guitar known
as a *vihuela* to produce traditional folk
music which is a romantic blend of
European and native American
influences. We wanted to create a
cocktail that honored the *mariachi*, so
we blended indigenous and foreign
ingredients in a drink that is vibrant,
strong, spicy, and full of character.

Chill a Martini glass. Place the chili pepper
in a cocktail shaker and muddle with the
flat end of a bar spoon. Add the remaining
ingredients. Fill with cubed ice and shake
well. Double strain into the Martini glass.
Dust with smoked paprika and serve.

GLASS Martini
GARNISH thin slice cucumber
4 slices cucumber
3 slices fresh fennel
Dash sugar syrup
1³/₄oz (50ml) blanco tequila (Don Julio)
2 teaspoons Cointreau
2 teaspoons fresh lemon juice

CUCUMBER AND FENNEL MARGARITA

Cucumber and fennel are often paired
in Middle Eastern cuisine to
produce wonderfully fresh salad and
rice dishes. We've combined them here
to similar effect, resulting in an
astoundingly vibrant Margarita which
leaves a lingering spiciness on the
back palate. It makes an ideal aperitif as
it lightly challenges all your taste buds,
waking them up prior to a meal.

Chill a Martini glass. Place the cucumber,
fennel, and sugar syrup in a cocktail shaker. Muddle well with the flat end of a bar
spoon or the end of a rolling pin. Add the
remaining ingredients. Fill with cubed ice
and shake well. Double strain into the
Martini glass. Float a slice of cucumber on
top and serve.

GLASS hurricane
GARNISH melon ball
1³/₄oz (50ml) plata tequila (Patrón Silver)
¹/₂oz (15ml) honey
6 dice-sized chunks galia melon
2 teaspoons Greek yogurt
2¹/₂oz (75ml) cloudy apple juice
¹/₂oz (15ml) ginseng jelly

POWER PUNCH

A cocktail packed with goodness and vitality. Look for ginseng in your local Chinese grocery or health-food store. Ginseng is a natural superfood, defending the body from physical strain, boosting mental activity, and—by stimulating the endocrine glands—possibly even acting as an aphrodisiac!

Place all the ingredients in a blender with a cup of crushed ice. Blend for 30 seconds. Pour directly into a hurricane glass (no need to strain). For the garnish use a melon baller to make a melon ball or cut a small triangle of melon and float on top. Serve.

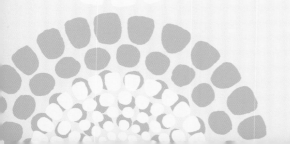

GLASS	³/₄oz (25ml) agave syrup (or sugar syrup)
Martini	Bunch fresh rosemary
	1³/₄oz (50ml) plata tequila (Gran Centenario)
GARNISH	¹/₂oz (15ml) Cointreau
fresh rosemary sprig	³/₄oz (25ml) fresh lime juice

Rosa Maria

This mix marries the strong Mediterranean influences
of rosemary with the sweet, spicy notes of tequila to offer you
a dense and flavorsome experience. Although rosemary
grows in abundance all year round in many areas, its flavor
is restricted in colder months and places, so be prepared to
experiment with this recipe and adjust the amount of
rosemary to suit your taste. You'll notice that we've used a
little more sweetener than usual in this one. This is to counteract
the woody, tannic elements of the rosemary, which can produce
a bitter aftertaste. Overall this can be a tricky one to get right,
but well worth it once you've succeeded!

Chill a Martini glass. Place the rosemary and agave syrup in a cocktail shaker and muddle with the flat end of a bar spoon or the end of a rolling pin. Add the remaining ingredients and shake well. Double strain into the Martini glass. Float a sprig of fresh rosemary on the top and serve.

FRESH &
Fruity

You don't need an excuse for a Margarita, but
with all the fresh fruit in these mouthwatering
recipes, you'll feel even better about drinking
them. Packed with ingredients like apples and
pears, summer berries, and tropical delights,
these refreshing fruit-flavors are perfect for
long, lazy days and warm, summer nights.

GLASS	1 pomegranate
Martini	1^1/$_2$oz (45ml) reposado tequila (El Charro)
	2 teaspoons Cointreau
GARNISH	^{1}/$_2$oz (15ml) fresh lime juice
half salt and	1 teaspoon Grenadine
sugar rim	

POMEGRANATE MARGARITA

In this mix the smokiness of reposado tequila is balanced by the intense orange flavor of Cointreau, but you could use a different triple sec if you prefer. To save time you can substitute the pomegranate for ^{3}/$_4$oz (25ml) pomegranate juice, but the fresh stuff gives the best results. Take care to use plastic gloves and an apron when handling pomegranates as the juice can stain. We know this one might sound a little like hard work, but we assure you it's worth it; it's a perfect slow-sipper that gets you pretty close to heaven.

Cut the pomegranate into quarters and scoop all the seeds and flesh into a small bowl. Place a sieve on top of your cocktail shaker. Transfer the seeds and flesh into the sieve and press through with the back of a spoon. Add the remaining ingredients. Fill with cubed ice and shake well. To coat the rim crush together equal proportions of rock salt and granulated white sugar in a pestle and mortar. Wipe only half the rim with lime and dip in the salt–sugar mix. Double strain the drink into the glass, taking care not to let any of the salt–sugar mix fall into the drink. Serve.

1³/₄oz (50ml) plata tequila (Patrón Silver)
¹/₂oz (15ml) fresh lime juice
¹/₂oz (15ml) agave syrup (or treacle)
5 dice-sized cubes watermelon

GLASS
Martini

GARNISH
watermelon triangle

Melonrita

This is a variation on the contemporary classic Vodka Watermelon Martini. We find tequila to be a superior base ingredient as its pepperiness works beautifully with the light fruitiness of fresh watermelon. Here we're using a neutral-style silver tequila which works well with fresh fruit flavors. Agave syrup binds the ingredients as well as providing a hint of treacle to the overall experience. But real treacle makes a satisfactory substitute. Serve in a hollowed-out half of watermelon with four long straws for a sociable summer Margarita—great for barbecues!

Chill a Martini glass. Place the diced watermelon and agave syrup in a cocktail shaker. Crush gently with the flat end of a bar spoon to form a pulp. Pour in the remaining ingredients. Fill with cubed ice and shake well. Double strain into the Martini glass. Slide the watermelon triangle onto the rim and serve.

GLASS Martini

GARNISH red currants on the stalk

1³/₄oz (50ml) blanco tequila (Don Julio)

¹/₂oz (15ml) elderflower cordial

³/₄oz (25ml) clear apple juice

Dash fresh lime juice

GLASS champagne flute

GARNISH none

³/₄oz (25ml) añejo tequila (1800)

1³/₄oz (50ml) grape and honey purée

  (see below)

¹/₂ cup (100ml) prosecco

Elderflower Margarita

We've replaced the traditional orange and lime flavors with apple and elderflower to produce an exceptionally delicate Margarita reminiscent of an English country garden. For best results use a tequila with fresh notes, such as Don Julio Blanco or Gran Centenario Plata.

Chill a Martini glass. Pour all the ingredients into a cocktail shaker. Fill with cubed ice and shake well. Double strain into the glass. Hang a small stalk of red currants on the rim and serve.

Uva y Miel

A Bellini-style drink that packs an extra punch. The intense flavors of the grape and honey are best complemented by a rich tequila like 1800 Añejo, with its hints of caramel and oak. It's a recipe that requires a little bit of preparation, but it's well worth the effort for a sophisticated cocktail soirée.

Chill a champagne flute. Pour all the ingredients into a mixing glass. Stir gently until the ingredients combine. Don't stir too much or you'll remove the fizz. Pour (no need to strain) and serve.

TRICKS AND TIPS

For the grape and honey purée, wash and de-stalk a large bunch of red seedless grapes. Place in a blender. Add 1 cup (225ml) honey and ³/₄ cup (175ml) hot, but not boiling, water. Blend for around a minute. Allow to cool then press through a coarse sieve. Covered and refrigerated, this keeps for around five days.

GLASS champagne flute
GARNISH none

³/₄oz (25ml) plata tequila (El Charro Silver)
³/₄oz (25ml) apricot purée (see below)
³/₄oz (25ml) pink grapefruit juice
1 teaspoon agave syrup (or sugar syrup)
¹/₂ cup (100ml) prosecco

Sombrero

We had to name at least one for the extravagant Mexican headgear. This is another fruity glass of fizz, in which a smooth El Charro Silver is a perfect counterfoil for all those bubbles. If you can't find prosecco use any sparkling wine as long as it's dry— sweet wine might make it taste sickly.

Chill a champagne flute. Pour all the ingredients into a mixing glass. Stir gently until combined. Don't stir too much or you'll remove the fizz. Pour (no need to strain) and serve.

TRICKS AND TIPS

To make any of the fruit purées, simply peel the fruit and remove any inedible parts such as the stalk or seeds. Place in a blender, add 1 to 2 teaspoons sugar or agave syrup, to taste. Blend for a minute. If the fruit isn't very juicy, add a little more sweetener. Cover and refrigerate. Keeps for around a week.

1¹/₂oz (45ml) reposado tequila (Gran Centenario)
2 teaspoons Chambord
1 blackberry
2 raspberries
3 strawberries
4 blueberries
1 tablespoon superfine (caster) sugar
³/₄oz (25ml) fresh lime juice

GLASS
hurricane or
large wine glass

GARNISH
sugar rim and
one of each berry

Many Berry Margarita

Chambord is a rich raspberry liqueur with notes of herbs and honey that beautifully complements the tang of summer fruits. But you can substitute it with any fruit liqueur if you prefer. This mouthwatering concoction is best combined with a sweet, full-bodied reposado such as Gran Centenario to make a lovely, slushy Margarita that will keep you cool when lazing by the pool.

Place all the ingredients in a blender with a cup of crushed ice. Blend for around 30 seconds until the mix achieves a sorbet-like consistency. Wipe the rim of a hurricane glass with a strawberry, then dip in a saucer of superfine sugar. Single strain the mix into the glass. Pierce one of each berry with a cocktail stick, rest the stick on the rim, and serve.

GLASS	1³/₄oz (50ml) plata tequila (Gran Centenario)
old-fashioned	2 teaspoons Cointreau
	³/₄oz (25ml) pink grapefruit juice
GARNISH	¹/₂oz (15ml) fresh lemon juice
grapefruit zest	2 teaspoons orange marmalade
	1 teaspoon agave syrup (or sugar syrup)

Morning Margarita

If you want to impress a breakfast guest, why not serve this Margarita in a hollowed-out grapefruit half, accompanied by a side of hot, buttered toast? When pouring there's no need to double strain, as the flecks of lemon and grapefruit and tiny chunks of sweet marmalade give it a bit of bite— the perfect morning pick-me-up.

Place all the ingredients in a cocktail shaker in the order listed above. Fill with cubed ice and shake well, until the marmalade has fully broken up into the drink. Fill an old-fashioned glass with cubed ice. Single strain the mix over the ice. Finish with a sprinkling of thin strips of grapefruit zest and serve.

1¹/₄oz (35ml) reposado tequila (Jose Cuervo Tradicional)
¹/₂oz (15ml) Agavero (tequila liqueur)
1 passion fruit
¹/₂oz (15ml) fresh lime juice
2 teaspoons vanilla sugar (see below)
³/₄oz (25ml) cloudy apple juice

GLASS
tall

GARNISH
apple fan

La Cucaracha

This **exotic** libation was created by the wonderful **Douglas Ankrah**, legendary coctelero, cocktail writer, and **raconteur** from ole' London Town. Douglas originally made this drink for one of his **many lovers**, a Mexican girl, who was often heard shouting after him "you're nothing but a *cucaracha!*" *Cucaracha* is Spanish for **cockroach**.

Half fill a tall glass with crushed ice. Add all the ingredients, slicing the passion fruit in half and scooping the flesh and edible seeds into the glass. Stir well. Fill to the rim with more crushed ice. To garnish cut one green and one red apple into crescent-shaped slices. Form a fan shape with alternating slices of green and red apple and slide into the side of the glass. Serve.

TRICKS AND TIPS

To make vanilla sugar, fill a glass jar or bowl with 2 cups (400g) granulated sugar. Split a vanilla bean lengthwise and crosswise and place in the sugar. Mix well. The vanilla will impart the sugar with a strong flavor in minutes. You can leave the bean in the sugar for up to two weeks. After that, the vanilla will start to dry out and give the sugar a more bitter flavor. Vanilla sugar tastes wonderful sprinkled over baked goods, cappuccinos, or fruit.

GLASS hurricane
GARNISH dusting of ground nutmeg
              and lime wedge
1^3/$_4$oz (50ml) reposado tequila
    (Gran Centenario)
^{1}/$_2$ banana, sliced
1^3/$_4$oz (50ml) pineapple juice
1^3/$_4$oz (50ml) mango juice
^{3}/$_4$oz (25ml) fresh lime juice
^{3}/$_4$oz (25ml) coconut syrup

NIÑA COLADA

A wonderfully exotic concoction, based on the traditional Piña Colada but with additional fruitiness in the form of banana and mango. We created this one for our friend Nina Ferguson, a brilliant event organizer and dedicated cocktail connoisseur.

Chill a hurricane glass. Place all the ingredients in a blender in the order listed above. Add a cup of crushed ice. Blend well for around 30 seconds. Pour directly into the glass (no need to strain). Dust the surface with ground nutmeg, push a lime wedge on the rim, and serve.

GLASS highball or tall
GARNISH papaya slice
^{1}/$_2$ medium papaya
1^3/$_4$oz (50ml) reposado tequila
    (Sauza Hornitos)
^{3}/$_4$oz (25ml) fresh lime juice
^{1}/$_2$oz (15ml) coconut syrup
1^3/$_4$oz (50ml) cloudy apple juice

PAPAYA, LIME, AND COCONUT

Papayas are grown in Mexico where they reach enormous proportions, measuring up to 15 inches (40cm). But the type that you see in your local grocery store is much more likely to be the smaller, sweeter Hawaiian papaya. Adding lime to papaya has a magical effect, bringing the papaya flavor alive; try squeezing a little lime juice on a slice and you'll see what we mean. Overall, this is an intensely fruity concoction with a background of spice from the tequila. Delicious!

Scoop the flesh and seeds out of the papaya into a blender. Add the remaining ingredients. Blend (without ice) for about 30 seconds, until smooth. Half fill a highball or tall glass with crushed ice and pour the mix over the ice (no need to strain). Rest a papaya slice on the rim and serve.

GLASS tall
GARNISH lime wedge
1³/₄oz (50ml) plata tequila (1800 Silver)
1 teaspoon agave syrup (or sugar syrup)
Dash fresh lime juice
4 oz (100ml) pink grapefruit juice
¹/₂ cup (100ml) soda water

PALOMA

Ask for a Paloma (meaning "dove") in
an American bar and you'll probably be
met with confusion, but in most bars in
Mexico the bartender will know this
cocktail—try it when you're next
visiting and you'll be recognized as
slightly more discriminating than
the average tourist. Called a Fresca in
some regions, you could describe the
Paloma as a carbonated Margarita.
It's similar in taste, but a little faster to
make. Whereas it can be difficult to find
a well-prepared Margarita, you'll find
that a Paloma consistently hits the
spot. It's become one of our favorite
tequila cocktails for making at home.

Fill a tall glass with cubed ice. Build the
ingredients over the ice in the order listed
above. Stir briefly. Drop a lime wedge in the
glass and serve.

GLASS	1³/₄oz (50ml) añejo tequila (Don Julio)
Martini	³/₄oz (25ml) pineapple juice
	¹/₂oz (15ml) Cherry Heering (or any cherry liqueur)
GARNISH	
lipstick kiss	

The Playboy

The Playboy may be a bit of fun but it has surprising depth of character and sophistication. The exceptionally smooth and rich Don Julio Añejo is the perfect choice for this mix. It's a top-of-the-range tequila named after the great Don Julio González, who began running his own distillery at the age of 17 and whose wealth of experience ensures that only the best agave plants are used in his spirits. To finish the cocktail, the pineapple juice froths up to create a velvety texture that is exceptionally sensuous when passing your lips! If the lipstick kiss isn't your thing, a tequila-soaked cherry is a more traditional garnish.

Chill a Martini glass. Pour all the ingredients into a cocktail shaker in the order listed above. Fill with cubed ice and shake well. Single strain into the Martini glass. Kiss and serve.

100% FACT

Another claimant for inventing the Margarita (see also page 26) was the wealthy socialite, Margarita Sames. In 1948 she was hosting a party at her vacation home in Acapulco, Mexico, when she invented a cocktail using the native spirit, tequila. Her guests loved it so much they took the recipe back to Hollywood, where it spread through the glitterati like wildfire.

GLASS old-fashioned
GARNISH orange strips and
   2 raspberries

4 raspberries

$^1/_4$ orange, chopped

2 heaped teaspoons light brown
   (Demerara) sugar

1$^3/_4$oz (50ml) reposado tequila
   (Gran Centenario)

2 teaspoons fresh lemon juice

MASSO

We created this fruity version of the Caipirinha—a mix of lime, sugar, and Brazilian rum—in honor of Andres' mother. This extraordinary woman spent many years working in a fresh juice and soft drink factory in Colombia, where she mastered the art of combining fruit flavors. It's a skill that her son is proud to inherit.

Place the raspberries, orange segments, and sugar in the base of an old-fashioned glass. Using the flat end of a bar spoon muddle to form a pulp. Add crushed ice (fill the glass around halfway). Add the tequila and lemon juice. Stir well. Add more crushed ice to fill to the rim. Float small strips of orange zest and two raspberries on the top and serve.

GLASS champagne flute
GARNISH thin mango slice
Dash absinthe (or Pernod)
1³/₄oz (50ml) añejo tequila (Herradura)
2¹/₂oz (75ml) mango purée (see page 69)
¹/₂oz (15ml) fresh lime juice
1 teaspoon agave syrup (or sugar syrup)

LAST MANGO IN PARIS

A taste of illicit pleasure, named for the notoriety of one of its ingredients: absinthe. The emerald-green liqueur was the tipple of choice among artists and writers in Parisian cafés until it was banned in France and the USA in the early 20th century, amid unproven fears it could cause dependency. Absinthe is legal, however, in the UK and Canada. If you're in one of these countries, use absinthe, as it has a fabulous aniseed flavor. Elsewhere, Pernod or Herbsaint are good substitutes.

Pre-chill a champagne flute. Pour a dash of absinthe or Pernod into the flute, swill it around to coat the inside, then discard any excess. Place the remaining ingredients in a cocktail shaker. Fill with cubed ice and shake well. Single strain into the flute, drop in a slice of mango, and serve.

GLASSES champagne flutes
GARNISHES strawberry halves
4¹/₂oz (125ml) reposado tequila
   (El Charro)
1oz (30ml) sugar syrup
1oz (30ml) crème de fraise
8oz (225g) fresh strawberries
1 bottle cava

FRESA FIZZ

Strawberries and bubbly—a mouthwatering combination. We've used plenty of fresh strawberries in this one, resulting in a delightful pink concoction. El Charro Reposado is perfect for this mix: its strength of character gives the mix a good tequila flavor. This recipe serves six, so is ideal for summer garden parties.

Chill the champagne flutes. Wash and de-hull the strawberries. Place in a blender with all the other ingredients except the cava. Blend thoroughly. Add the cava and stir. Pour into the champagne flutes (no need to strain). Place strawberry halves on the rims and serve.

½ thick slice pineapple
3 raspberries
2 teaspoons agave syrup (or sugar syrup)
1¾oz (50ml) reposado tequila (Herradura)
2 teaspoons fresh lemon juice

GLASS
old-fashioned

GARNISH
pineapple leaves and
a fresh raspberry

RASPBERRY AND PINEAPPLE SMASH

With its vibrant coloring and the small flecks of fruit pulp running through the glass, this concoction is very pleasing on the eye. We call it a "Smash" because of the way you mix it and the way it tastes: this is a refreshing Margarita with a wonderfully intense fruitiness. A taste of this and you'll be transported all the way to the porch of a Mexican hacienda.

Chop the pineapple slice into small chunks and transfer to a mixing glass. Add the fresh raspberries and agave syrup. Muddle with the flat end of a bar spoon or the end of a rolling pin. Half fill with crushed ice. Add the remaining ingredients and stir well. Pour into the old-fashioned glass and fill to the rim with crushed ice. Slide two pineapple leaves into the side of the glass, float a raspberry on the top, and serve.

100% FACT

If you're in Mexico and you have a few too many Margaritas, you might be offered the traditional hangover cure of *menudo*. However, as this fatty stew consists of hot chili pepper, tripe, and calves' hooves, it may be better to avoid drinking too much in the first place!

SWEET
Indulgence

Sometimes you need a touch of something
rich, velvety, and naughty. So go on, spoil
yourself with these deliciously sweet and
sophisticated dessert mixes. Serve them to friends
as an after-dinner treat or keep them all to
yourself as a luxurious self-indulgence.

GLASS	1¼oz (35ml) reposado tequila (El Tesoro)
Martini	2 teaspoons caramel liqueur
	2 teaspoons pineapple juice
GARNISH	½oz (15ml) fresh lime juice
half salt and	Dash sugar syrup
sugar rim	

Caramelo

Ideally served as an **after-dinner cocktail**, this is also a fantastic introduction to Margaritas for those who find the authentic recipe too tart and zesty. We recommend El Tesoro Reposado as the base spirit because it provides **smoky** and **peppery** characteristics which interact perfectly with the sweetness of the pineapple and caramel. This smokiness is achieved by specially selecting **perfectly ripe** agaves from specific areas. A salt and sugar rim perfectly shows off all the flavor profiles within the drink, but you could mix toffee flakes or crumbled chocolate with a little salt instead. For an even more luxurious variation, half fill a **champagne flute** with the mixture and charge it with chilled champagne.

Pour all the ingredients into a cocktail shaker in the order listed above. Fill with cubed ice and shake for about five seconds, until the pineapple is frothy and creamy. To coat the rim of the Martini glass, wipe half the rim with a piece of pineapple. Dip into a saucer of sea salt and granulated white sugar. Pour (no need to strain) and serve.

3¹/₂oz (100ml) añejo tequila (Patrón)
1³/₄oz (50ml) Frangelico
1³/₄oz (50ml) chocolate liqueur
¹/₂oz (15ml) agave syrup (or sugar syrup)

GLASSES
shots

GARNISHES
dark and white
chocolate shavings

Chocology

Frangelico, the original hazelnut liqueur, is produced in
the hills of the Piedmont area of Italy. Its origins date back to
Christian monks who lived here more than 300 years ago.
They were skilled in the arts of distillation, and based their recipes
on local ingredients, including wild hazelnuts. The liqueur was
named for Friar Angelico, a legendary hermit monk. This
densely flavored cocktail—ideally suited to chocolatey
Patrón Añejo—is the perfect end to a well-planned meal.
The recipe makes four shots—enough to share with friends.

Chill four shot glasses. Pour all the
ingredients into a cocktail shaker. Fill
with cubed ice and shake well. Single
strain into the glasses. Grate some dark
and white chocolate over the top of the
drinks. Serve.

GLASS
old-fashioned

GARNISH
shredded
coconut rim

1¹/₂oz (45ml) plata tequila (Patrón Silver)
2 teaspoons crème de menthe (white)
2 teaspoons coconut cream

CoCo LoCo

A sweet but intensely flavored cocktail with the beautifully cool pairing of mint and coconut. To preserve its clean look use colorless white crème de menthe rather than the green version. If you want to emphasize the tropical theme, try serving this in half an empty coconut shell.

Pour all the ingredients into a cocktail shaker in the order listed above. Fill with cubed ice and shake well. Wipe the rim of an old-fashioned glass with a little coconut cream and dip into a saucer of shredded coconut. Single strain the drink into the glass and serve.

GLASS champagne flute
GARNISH none
1³/₄oz (50ml) blanco tequila (Herradura)
1³/₄oz (50ml) peach purée (see page 69)
Dash crème de pêche
Dash fresh lemon juice
³/₄oz (25ml) heavy (double) cream

GLASS Martini
GARNISH lemon twist
1¹/₄oz (35ml) reposado tequila (Herradura)
¹/₂oz (15ml) limoncello
³/₄oz (25ml) fresh lemon juice
2 teaspoons vanilla sugar (see page 75)

PEACHES AND CREAM

Juicy and creamy all at once, this drink is lip-smackingly good! Use Herradura Blanco if you can; its floral and caramel notes blend beautifully with the fragrance of peach—the aroma of summer orchards.

Chill a champagne flute. Pour all the ingredients into a cocktail shaker. Fill with cubed ice and shake well. Double strain the mix into the flute and serve.

LEMON SHERBET

If you've ever been to Italy you've probably tasted limoncello. The lemon liqueur is regularly served ice cold in the hot summer months. Authentic limoncello is made from the rinds of Sorrento lemons, which are soaked in pure alcohol for 90 days. With the addition of sugar and water you have limoncello. You can actually make something similar at home using vodka.

Chill a Martini glass. Place all the ingredients in a cocktail shaker. Fill with cubed ice and shake well. Double strain into the Martini glass. Using a sharp knife or lemon zester, pare off a long, thin strip of lemon zest, and drop into the drink. Serve.

GLASS large old-fashioned
GARNISH cookie crumbs
1³/₄oz (50ml) reposado tequila
   (Gran Centenario)
¹/₂oz (15ml) cinnamon sugar (see page 96)
1³/₄oz (50ml) apple purée (see page 69)
1³/₄oz (50ml) cloudy apple juice
Dash fresh lime juice
³/₄oz (25ml) heavy (double) cream

APPLE CRUMBLE

Based on the traditional English dessert, this is an ideal cocktail to serve in colder climes as night falls and the fires need lighting. Tequila and lime give an additional lift to the scrumptious combination of apple, cinnamon, and cream.

Chill an old-fashioned glass. Pour all the ingredients except the cream into a cocktail shaker. Fill with cubed ice and shake well. Fill the old-fashioned glass with fresh cubed ice. Single strain the mixture over the ice. Rest the flat end of a bar spoon on the surface and slowly pour the cream down the twisted handle so that it forms a thin layer on top of the drink. Sprinkle the cookie crumbs on the surface and serve.

1 fresh fig	**GLASS**
1$^1/_2$ teaspoons honey	**Martini**
1$^1/_2$ teaspoons hot water	
1$^3/_4$oz (50ml) reposado tequila (El Tesoro)	**GARNISH**
$^3/_4$oz (25ml) fresh lime juice	**none**

Fig and Honey Nectar

The delicate sweetness of fresh figs married with the mellow earthiness of reposado tequila—this is truly a drink for the gods. Its richness and intensity make great accompaniments for cheese or desserts. Sip and savor this nectar, as there are many sides to its character.

Chill a Martini glass. Wash the fig and remove the hard portion of the stem. Peel and cut into small pieces. Transfer to a cocktail shaker. Add the honey and water and muddle with the flat end of a bar spoon or the end of a rolling pin. Add the remaining ingredients. Fill with cubed ice and shake well. Single strain into the Martini glass and serve.

GLASS	1³/₄oz (50ml) plata tequila (Gran Centenario)
tall or sling	1³/₄oz (50ml) pear purée (see page 69)
	2 teaspoons cinnamon sugar (see below)
GARNISH	2 teaspoons crème de mûre
blackberry	¹/₂ cup (100ml) prosecco

PEAR AND CINNAMON MARGARITA

This is loosely based on the Bellini cocktail, created in the '30s by Giuseppi Cipriani at Harry's Bar, Venice. Cipriani named the Bellini in honor of the 15th-century painter, as the peaches and pinks in the cocktail reminded Cipriani of the colors in Bellini's work. Although many people make Bellinis with champagne, the original recipe used prosecco, a dry, sparkling wine from northern Italy. In our version the light wine combines perfectly with the richer fruity flavors of pear and blackberry.

Chill a tall or sling glass. Pour all the ingredients except the prosecco into a cocktail shaker. Fill with cubed ice and shake well. Half fill the tall or sling glass with crushed ice and pour the drink over the ice (no need to strain). Top up with prosecco, adding more ice if required. Float a blackberry on the top and serve.

TRICKS AND TIPS

For cinnamon sugar, fill a glass jar or bowl with 2 cups (400g) granulated sugar. Place one or two sticks of cinnamon in the container and mix well. The sticks will infuse the sugar with a cinnamon flavor in around a week. Alternatively, mix 1 cup (200g) granulated sugar with 2 teaspoons ground cinnamon in a dry blender. Sprinkle on baked goods, coffees, or fruit.

4 to 5 drops Angostura bitters
1 teaspoon white sugar
1³/₄oz (50ml) añejo tequila (Don Julio)
1 long strip of orange peel

GLASS
brandy balloon

GARNISH
none

Bermejo Blazer

In making this cocktail you're essentially producing your very own tequila liqueur by sweetening, flavoring, and semi-cooking the base spirit. Take the time to enjoy the wonderful and intense aromas. This is best served in front of an open log fire after a hard day skiing—James Bond eat your heart out!

Pre-warm the tequila by placing the bottle in a large basin or jug of hot water. Fill a small bowl with boiling water and rest the brandy balloon on top of the bowl until the glass is warm. Add the sugar and bitters to the base of the glass and press together gently with the back of a bar spoon until they form a paste. Add the tequila. Continue to steam heat the glass over the bowl while stirring. Holding an orange over the glass, pare off a long, continuous strip of zest, releasing the aromatic oils into the glass. Drop the twist in the glass and continue to heat for about one minute.

Finally the blazing. Carefully tilt the warmed glass on the bowl so that the liquid reaches the rim. Point the open end of the glass away from your face and light the top of the liquid with a match. The flame will be very pale and last for about 5 to 10 seconds. Place a saucer on the top of the glass to extinguish the flame and serve. Don't drink it immediately, as the rim will be extremely hot—if you prefer transfer it to a fresh brandy balloon. There is nothing worse than burnt lips; you wouldn't be able to kiss for ages!

GLASS
old-fashioned

GARNISH
raisins and
cinnamon flakes

1¹/₄oz (35ml) reposado tequila (Patrón)
¹/₂oz (15ml) butterscotch schnapps
2 teaspoons passion fruit syrup
³/₄oz (25ml) milk
³/₄oz (25ml) light (single) cream

Cookies and Cream

Silky tones of butterscotch and passion fruit balance harmoniously with the richness of tequila, milk, and cream. Substitute passion fruit syrup for any exotic fruit syrup if you prefer; the end result is still a luscious libation tasting of mamma's homemade cookies. Lock the door, curl up on the sofa, and enjoy!

Pour all the ingredients into a cocktail shaker. Fill with cubed ice and shake well. Fill the old-fashioned glass with fresh cubed ice and single strain the mix over the ice. Skewer a few large raisins on a cocktail stick and place on top. Finish with a sprinkling of crumbled cinnamon stick (or chocolate if you prefer) and serve.

GLASS old-fashioned
GARNISH raspberry
1³/₄oz (50ml) plata tequila (Patrón Silver)
³/₄oz (25ml) milk
³/₄oz (25ml) heavy (double) cream
2 teaspoons sugar syrup
2 teaspoons Chambord

GLASS Martini
GARNISH raspberry
1¹/₄oz (35ml) plata tequila
  (Gran Centenario)
2 teaspoons crème fraîche
³/₄oz (25ml) limoncello
2 teaspoons mango syrup
3 raspberries
³/₄oz (25ml) pink grapefruit juice

Neapolitan

We had to call this one a Neapolitan because it looks so much like the triple-colored ice cream. Sip it slowly and you'll notice that it tastes pretty similar, too: the Chambord includes flavors of raspberry and honeyed vanilla, while the Patrón Silver gives it a chocolatey finish (with a little bit of marzipan on top).

Half fill an old-fashioned glass with crushed ice. Add all the ingredients except the Chambord. Stir well. Add more crushed ice to fill almost to the rim. Gently pour the Chambord over the top using a circular motion so that you create a ripple effect bleeding through the drink. Float a raspberry on the surface and serve.

Angelita

The inspiration for this came from a Sunday lunch prepared by our friend Coelina. She finished off the meal by serving a dessert of raspberries, fresh mango, and chunks of pink grapefruit, drizzled with lime juice and topped with crème fraiche. We provided the tequila—Gran Centenario Plata, beautiful for sipping.

Chill a Martini glass. Place all the ingredients in a cocktail shaker. Fill with cubed ice and shake well. Double strain into the Martini glass. Float a raspberry on the surface and serve.

GLASS old-fashioned
GARNISH dried chamomile buds
1³/₄oz (50ml) reposado tequila
  (Gran Centenario)
1oz (30ml) chamomile tea mix (see below)
2 teaspoons fresh lime juice
2 teaspoons fresh lemon juice

Goodnight Margarita

This soothing libation was created by the bartending professor Charles Vexenat. Chamomile makes a pleasant aromatic tea which is said to soothe aches and pains, as well as naturally promoting restful sleep.

Chill an old-fashioned glass. Place all the ingredients in a cocktail shaker. Fill with cubed ice and shake well. Double strain into the old-fashioned glass. Float some chamomile buds on the surface and serve.

TRICKS AND TIPS

For the tea mix, place 10 chamomile teabags in 3 cups (750ml) boiling water and leave to steep for 10 minutes. Remove the teabags and add 1 cup (225ml) agave syrup. Heat the mix in a pan over a low heat for five minutes, then leave to cool. Covered and refrigerated this keeps around 10 days.

GLASS	6 raspberries
tall or highball	¹/₂oz (15ml) agave syrup (or sugar syrup)
	1¹/₄oz (35ml) reposado tequila (Gran Centenario)
GARNISH	¹/₂oz (15ml) Chambord
raspberry and	1³/₄oz (50ml) red cranberry juice
lime strips	³/₄oz (25ml) fresh lime juice

ESTES

This cocktail is named for Tomas Estes, official Ambassador of Tequila for Europe and owner of the fabulous Café Pacifico restaurants in London, Paris, Amsterdam, and Sydney. With their innovative tequila cocktails, great Mexican cuisine, and warm welcome, Café Pacificos are favorite haunts for the world's top bartenders and others "in the know."

Place the raspberries and agave syrup in the base of a tall or highball glass and crush with the flat end of a bar spoon. Add crushed ice almost to the rim, then add the remaining ingredients in the order listed above. Stir well. Top up with more crushed ice if necessary. Using a sharp knife or lemon zester, pare some short, thin strips of lime zest. Float them on top of the drink, add a fresh raspberry, and serve.

1½oz (45ml) plata tequila (Gran Centenario)
2 teaspoons Kahlúa
1 teaspoon sugar syrup
1 single espresso, freshly made

GLASS
Martini or
glass coffee cup

GARNISH
3 coffee beans

Jalisco Espress

This **velvety smooth concoction** makes a delicious after-dinner cocktail or even a cheeky breakfast alternative. It's essential that you use a **freshly made coffee**, not only for reasons of **flavor**, but also because when shaken it creates a naturally **creamy foam** on top of the drink. **Gran Centenario** makes a good choice here, with its tones of **vanilla, caramel,** and **butterscotch**. If you can't get hold of Kahlúa, replace with any **coffee liqueur**.

Chill a Martini glass or coffee cup. Pour all the ingredients into a cocktail shaker. Fill with cubed ice and shake well. Single strain into the glass. Float the coffee beans on top and serve.

WITH
a twist

There's so much more you can do with a
Margarita than merely drink it. If you can't get
enough of your favorite tipple or you want to
impress some dinner guests, try these quirky but
quality food recipes. There are dips and nibbles
with a tequila kick, and delicious desserts
and ice pops—all strictly for grown-ups!

TO SERVE large serving dish and skewers
GARNISH none

1½oz (45ml) olive oil

4 chicken breasts, in bite-sized chunks

2 large onions, sliced

2 large cloves garlic, chopped

14oz (400g) can chopped tomatoes

⅔ cup (150ml) chicken stock

½ teaspoon dried mixed herbs

Salt and ground black pepper to taste

2 red bell peppers, sliced

1 small chili pepper, chopped

12 stuffed green olives, halved

4oz (120ml) reposado tequila

POLLO MEXICANO

Chunks of chicken in a spicy sauce, this dipping dish is great for sharing. Serve with skewers, hunks of bread to mop up the sauce, and plenty of napkins!

Heat the oil in a large pan and brown the chicken, around 3 to 4 minutes. Set aside.

Add the onions and garlic to the pan and fry 5 minutes. Add the tomatoes, stock, herbs, seasoning, bell peppers, and chili pepper. Return the chicken to the pan. Cover and simmer for about 30 minutes, until the chicken is tender. Transfer the chicken to a serving dish and keep warm.

Remove the pan from the heat. Allow the sauce to cool for 10 minutes. Transfer to a food processor and blend, holding the lid.

Rinse the pan, then reheat the sauce. Season if required. Remove from the heat and stir in the olives and tequila. Pour the sauce over the chicken. Stir and serve.

TO SERVE small bowl
GARNISH cilantro (coriander)

5 medium-sized tomatoes, halved

6 to 8 garlic cloves, not peeled

1 medium onion, peeled and quartered

4 to 6 small chili peppers (to taste)

1 small bunch cilantro (coriander)

2 teaspoons kosher salt

1oz (30ml) fresh lime juice

2oz (60ml) reposado tequila

Sea salt to taste

4 to 5 drops Tabasco sauce (optional)

SPICY SALSA

A spicy Mexican salsa to serve with tacos. Don't pulverize this in the blender after you've added the tomatoes—you want to maintain a chunky texture.

Place the tomatoes, garlic cloves, onion, and chili peppers on a griddle pan over medium heat. Char lightly all over and transfer to a bowl as they finish. Allow to cool. Peel the tomatoes and garlic. Remove the stalks of the chili peppers.

Place the garlic, chili peppers, cilantro, salt, and lime juice in a blender. Pulse repeatedly—stopping and scraping the sides—until finely chopped.

Add the tequila and tomatoes and pulse gently, just enough to break them up. Transfer to a non-metallic bowl.

Finely chop the onion and stir into the salsa. Season with salt and Tabasco, if desired. Cover and leave to stand at room temperature for one hour before serving.

TO SERVE small plate and dish
GARNISH none
For the crudités:
1 bunch scallions (spring onions)
1 red bell pepper
4oz (100g) baby carrots
4oz (100g) baby corn
For the vinaigrette:
1oz (30ml) plata tequila
1 teaspoon maple syrup
1½ teaspoons mustard powder
½oz (15ml) cider vinegar
1oz (30ml) cranberry juice
Sea salt to taste
½ cup (100ml) canola oil (or walnut oil)

MARGARITA CRUDITÉS

Raw, bite-sized vegetables make refreshing drinking nibbles. We've suggested some of our favorite vegetables, but use any raw vegetables you like. Serves four.

Wash the scallions, bell peppers, and carrots, and slice into bite-sized chunks. Wash the baby corn. Arrange all the vegetables on a serving plate.

In a bowl whisk together the tequila, maple syrup, mustard, vinegar, cranberry juice, and salt to taste. Add the oil in a stream, whisking until the oil emulsifies. Pour into a small serving dish. Serve immediately with the vegetables.

TO SERVE old-fashioned glass
GARNISH none
1 papaya
1 galia melon
1 mango
2½oz (75ml) plata tequila
1oz (30ml) triple sec
1oz (30ml) fresh lime juice
1 teaspoon fresh lemon juice
2 teaspoons sugar syrup

DRUNKEN FRUIT

We think the tang of the Margarita works amazingly with fresh mango, melon, and papaya, but you can use any fruit you like. Serves four.

Slice the fruit into bite-sized chunks and place in a sealable plastic container. Pour the remaining ingredients into a cocktail shaker. Fill with cubed ice and shake well. Single strain the Margarita over all the fruit. Seal the container and refrigerate for two hours. Transfer the fruit to an old-fashioned glass, and pour over any Margarita mix remaining at the bottom of the container. Serve.

TO SERVE 8 ice-pop molds and sticks
GARNISH none
1^1/$_4$lb (500g) strawberries, hulled and halved
^{1}/$_2$ cup (100ml) plata tequila
^{1}/$_2$ cup (100g) superfine (caster) sugar
^{1}/$_2$oz (15ml) fresh lime juice

STRAWBERRY MARGARITA ICE POPS

These Ice Pops are quick to make—around 10 minutes—but need to be prepared a day in advance. To make them non-alcoholic, substitute the tequila with freshly squeezed orange juice. Makes eight ice pops.

Place all the ingredients in a blender and blend until smooth. Press the mixture through a fine sieve into a non-metallic jug. Pour into molds and add sticks. Freeze for at least 24 hours.

TO SERVE Martini glass
**GARNISH red currants on the stalk and
    confectioner's (icing) sugar**
1^1/$_4$oz (35ml) plata tequila
^{1}/$_2$oz (15ml) triple sec
^{1}/$_2$oz (15ml) fresh lime juice
Dash fresh lemon juice
1 teaspoon sugar syrup
18oz (500ml) raspberry sorbet

RASPBERRY MARGARITA SORBET

There's no fuss with this one. Substitute raspberry sorbet for any flavor you like, homemade or bought from the store.

Pour all the ingredients except the sorbet into a cocktail shaker. Fill the shaker with cubed ice and shake well. Place the sorbet in a large mixing bowl. Pour the Margarita mix over the sorbet and stir well. Return to the freezer for one hour. Serve in a Martini glass topped with the red currants and a dusting of confectioners' sugar.

FLAVOR-MIX CHART

We're continually amazed at the versatility of tequila. There's no other spirit that combines so well with so many ingredients. Here we've picked out a few of the best and most accessible which you could use to create your own tequila cocktails. Keep an open mind when you mix: the best blends are often a complete surprise!

Apple Clean and refreshing. Combines well with dark soft berries. Release flavor by blending or muddling and shaking.

Banana Soft and sweet. Works with honey and tropical juices. Intensify richness with cream, yogurt, or coconut syrup. Must be blended.

Basil Sweet and pungent herb. Marries well with apple, pear, pineapple, and all citrus fruits, especially lemon. Rip to release aroma. Don't muddle too hard.

Caramel Luxurious and sweet. Adds color, richness, and depth. Combines well with pears and soft fruits, and berries.

Cardamom Bitter-sweet. Enhances sweet and savory dishes. Works well with deep, rich flavors, such as cherry, pineapple, and chocolate. Crush pods to release flavor.

Cherry Juicy, rich fruit. Good with other berries and nuts, particularly almonds. For best results remove stones, crush, and shake.

Chili pepper Hot, fiery spice. Goes well with most fruits. Use only in small amounts.

Chocolate Deep, rich, luxurious, and sexy. Combines well with fruits, coffee, and spices such as cinnamon and nutmeg. Add milk for smoothness. Best with reposado or añejo tequila.

Cilantro (coriander) Sweet herb with pungent, almost citrus, taste. Works in savory and sweet mixes. Most flavor is in the stalk.

Cinnamon Sweet, aromatic spice. Works with rich flavors and "winter" spices such as clove and star anise. Use in drink or as garnish.

Cloves Sharp, hot, and distinctive taste. Great for hot drinks like blazers and mulled wine. Press several into the flesh of soft fruit such as pear or peach and leave in a punch overnight for rich flavor.

Coconut Tropical, milky taste. Adds silky texture. Great with other exotic fruits such as mango or papaya. Works with all tequilas.

Coffee Rich, earthy, and dry. Benefits from a sweetener such as vanilla or butterscotch. For best results use a fresh espresso.

Cranberry Dry, yet refreshing. Use either juice or fruit (more bitter). Combine with soft berries or sweet grapes for a fuller flavor.

Cucumber Clean, subtle flavor. Works with strong spices and young tequila. Muddle and shake.

Cumin Strong-tasting spice. Goes well with chocolate and fresh fruit, particularly melon.

Dill Warm, mild anise flavor. Works well with intense tropical fruits and citrus.

Elderflower Sweet-tasting flower. Available as a cordial. Amazing with apple and a light tequila.

Fennel Seeds with a strong anise flavor. Great with cucumber and other delicate flavors. Only a small amount is required.

Ginger root Warm, biting flavor. Great with soda water and citrus fruits. Chop, smash, and shake for best results. Also available as cordial.

Grapefruit Bitter-sweet citrus fruit. Pink ones are sweeter. Add pinch of salt to enhance taste. Can be juiced or chopped and crushed.

Honey Sweet, treacle flavor and texture. Blends well with fruits and spices such as cinnamon and clove. Add hot water to dissolve.

Juniper Bitter-sweet tasting berries. Good for infusions (leave in a bottle of tequila for a week).

Lemongrass Strong lemon-flavor, with additional spice notes. Use only small amounts. Slice and smash for maximum effect. Strain well.

Mint Light, refreshing herb. Helps sweet flavors and citrus combine. Aromatic garnish.

Nutmeg Sweet, rich, warm spice. Works with fruity and creamy drinks. Use in drink or as garnish.

Paprika Smoky, and slightly sweet spice. Best with strong, rich flavors such as chocolate or pineapple. Use only small amounts.

Rosemary Woody and sweet herb. Use with sweet flavors, such as vanilla or caramel. Reduce bitterness by removing stalks.

Sage Strong, warm herb. Shake with fruit and tequila. Don't muddle too hard.

Tarragon Distinctive, fresh, aromatic herb. Works well with soft fruits and sweet flavors. Shows off the agave flavors of young tequilas.

Vanilla Rich, luxurious flavor. Combines well with all tequilas. Run a knife tip down the bean to release the seeds and the flavor.

INDEX BY INGREDIENTS

This index refers only to mixers that contribute significantly to the flavor of the cocktails.

INDEX ALPHABETICAL

ACKNOWLEDGMENTS

The authors would like to thank the following people for their help along the way, in no particular order: Kirsten and all at DBP; William Lingwood; Pacifico Posse; Breakfast Group; Lab legends & Loonies; Match Massive; Cotton House Crew; Dave Hobbs & Socio Rehab; Charles Vexenat; Danny Smith; Pablo El Gordo; Roy y Ramon (Guadalajara); Tequila Tour 2004; Col-di-Mura Massive; Dave Singh; La Capilla (Don Javier); Emily Wheldon; Gorgeous Group; IPB; Bar Total; Squeeze; Dick and Jenifer; Inspirit Brands; Terrell Twins; Plymouth Posse; Tres Agaves; San Francisco Sector (Eric, Dave, Marco, and Jacques); Simon Difford; Jasper and Cairbry; Nick Strangeway & Floridita Firm; Douglas; Rich and Goose; Tom and the Estes family; Trailer team; Charles and Adam Breeden; Lonsdale legends; Julio Bermejo y familia; Pedro "rocket scientist" Cervero; Lucy "angel" Hughes; Sue and Angus; Theme, Class, Flavour, and Playboy; Eric Rubin; Ricky Agnew at Marblehead; Ali B; Steve Blond; Oliver Peyton; Dave Steward; Ray and Nilsson; Ian Alexander; BLP PR (Eliot); Ian Wisniewski; Mark Ridgewell; Miranda Dickson; Lala and Radica; Mark and Cat; Ben Pundole; Nidal at Dusk; Ben Reed; Spike Marchant; Low-Life Dogs; Carlos Santana; Speedy Gonzalez!; Tom, Will, and Leo; JD and the Player Punks; Dale DeGroff; Audrey Saunders; Tony Abu Clanim; Phillip Wilson; Johnny La Plage; The Willcoxs; Stefano; Mark Pratt; Ruby (Dimi and Colin); Glenn and Angela; The Dodds; Nick Griffin and Pleisure; John Coe; Mark "ears" Dren; The Duggans; and mostly, the people of Mexico, all the members of the WCC ... and you!